Coyright © 2024

TABLE OF CONTENT

What is a Groundhog?

Groundhogs, also known as woodchucks, are fascinating creatures from the rodent family. They belong to a group called marmots and are closely related to squirrels. These furry animals typically measure 16 to 20 inches in length, including their bushy tails, which can add another 6 inches. A groundhog's body is covered in thick brown fur, which helps them blend into their environment and stay warm during colder months. Their powerful front claws and sharp teeth are perfect for digging and chewing, making them expert burrow builders.

Groundhogs are mostly found in North America, especially in areas with open fields, forests, and grassy regions. They thrive in places where they can dig burrows and find plenty of food. As herbivores, they love eating plants, including grass, clover, fruits, and vegetables. Sometimes, they even munch on flowers from gardens! Groundhogs can eat about one-third of their body weight in food every day, which helps them store energy for hibernation.

These animals are diurnal, meaning they are active during the day and rest at night. Groundhogs are known for their amazing digging skills and create complex underground homes called burrows. These burrows can have multiple entrances and rooms, including separate spaces for sleeping and storing food. A burrow can be up to 30 feet long! Groundhogs are also good climbers and swimmers, which helps them escape predators like foxes and hawks. Despite their shy nature, they are resilient and adaptable creatures.

Why Do Groundhogs Hibernate?

Hibernation is one of the most amazing things groundhogs do to survive the harsh winter months. When the temperature drops and food becomes scarce, groundhogs retreat to their burrows and enter a state of deep sleep called hibernation. This special adaptation allows them to conserve energy when they can't find enough food. During hibernation, their body slows down dramatically—breathing becomes slower, and their heartbeat can drop from about 80 beats per minute to just 5 beats! This helps them survive on the fat reserves they've built up during the warmer months.

Groundhogs prepare carefully for hibernation. Throughout the summer and fall, they eat a lot to gain weight and store fat. Their burrows, which are already cozy, are specially prepared for winter with extra insulation to keep them warm. The hibernation chamber is usually deep underground, where the temperature stays relatively stable and safe from predators. Once winter arrives, they curl up in their burrows, sleeping through the cold months and using very little energy.

Hibernation usually lasts from late fall until early spring, but groundhogs don't wake up all at once. In late winter, they may briefly emerge from their burrows to check the weather and look for signs of spring. When they finally end their hibernation, they're often thinner and hungry, so they immediately start foraging for food. This cycle of eating, storing fat, and hibernating is essential for their survival in cold climates. It's nature's way of helping these remarkable animals adapt to their environment.

Groundhog Day Fun Facts

Groundhog Day is a special tradition celebrated on February 2nd every year. The idea comes from an old belief: if a groundhog comes out of its burrow and sees its shadow, it means there will be six more weeks of winter. If it doesn't see its shadow, spring will arrive early. This fun event is celebrated in the United States and Canada, where people gather to see if the groundhog will "predict" the weather. While it's not scientifically accurate, the tradition is a delightful way to look forward to the changing seasons.

The most famous groundhog is Punxsutawney Phil, who lives in Pennsylvania. Every year, thousands of people visit Gobbler's Knob, a small hill where Phil makes his "prediction." The tradition dates back to 1887, and Phil has become a national celebrity! He even has his own group of caretakers called the Inner Circle, who dress in top hats and tuxedos during the event. Many other towns have their own groundhogs, like Wiarton Willie in Canada, but Phil remains the most well-known.

Groundhog Day might be fun and lighthearted, but it's also a reminder of the connection between humans and nature. The holiday comes from ancient European customs involving animals and weather predictions. Farmers used these signs to plan their planting and harvesting seasons. Today, Groundhog Day brings people together to celebrate the charm of this furry creature and the beauty of seasonal changes. It's a fun way to learn about the environment and appreciate the rhythms of nature.

How Groundhogs Help the Environment

Groundhogs are more than just cute animals; they play an important role in maintaining a healthy environment. One of the ways they help is through their digging. When groundhogs dig their burrows, they loosen and aerate the soil, which helps plants grow better. Their burrows can be very complex, with tunnels and chambers that can stretch up to 30 feet long. After a groundhog moves out, these burrows become homes for other animals, such as rabbits, foxes, and skunks, creating shelter and a safe space for different species.

Groundhogs are also great at spreading seeds, which helps new plants grow. When they eat fruits and vegetables, they unintentionally drop seeds in different areas as they travel. This helps plants spread and grow in new places, making the environment more diverse. Groundhogs' grazing habits can even help control the growth of certain plants, keeping ecosystems balanced and preventing any one type of plant from taking over.

In the bigger picture, groundhogs are an essential part of the food chain. Predators like foxes, coyotes, hawks, and owls rely on groundhogs as a source of food. By being a prey animal, groundhogs help these predators survive. This balance keeps ecosystems healthy and thriving. While groundhogs sometimes nibble on gardens and crops, their contributions to the environment far outweigh any trouble they might cause. They are a small but mighty part of the natural world, showing us how every creature has a role to play.

Made in United States
Troutdale, OR
01/20/2025